TWELVE SCENIC WALKS
FROM
THE NORTH YORKSHIRE MOORS
RAILWAY

by

J.Brian Beadle

First published in Great Britain in 2001 by Trailblazer Publishing (Scarborough)

www.trailblazerbooks.co.uk

ISBN   1   899004   39   4

Trailblazer Publishing (Scarborough)
Stoneways
South End
Burniston
Scarborough. YO13 0HP

MAPS
The maps in this book are not to scale and are for guidance only. They do not accurately portray the right of way. It is the readers responsibility not to stray from the right of way and it is strongly advised that you take the relevant Ordnance Survey map with you on the walk.

WARNING
Whilst every effort has been made for accuracy neither the publisher nor the author bear responsibility for the alteration, closure or portrayal of rights of way in this book. It is the readers responsibility not to invade private land or stray from the public right of way for walkers. All routes in the book should be treated with respect and all precautions taken before setting out. Any person using information in this book does so at their own risk. You must wear clothing and footwear suitable for rough and exposed walking.

CONTENTS

JUST A FEW WORDS

Walking from the North Yorkshire Moors Railway is certainly scenic as the name of the book implies. There is so much rich scenery alongside the railway line all the way from Pickering to Grosmont. You can see fabulous Newtondale from within the dale or from one of the many high cliffs and escarpments which surround this breathtaking haven hidden within the North York Moors. Standing high above the dale at the ruined Skelton Tower the steam trains below look like toys as they rattle and whistle their merry way between the trees of Cropton Forest. You can ask the guard to stop the train for you at the Newtondale Halt platform and as it pulls away from you peace and tranquility surrounds the dale, only the sounds of the receding train echoing from the cliffs. There are several great walks from the platform, the ones which climb high above the dale have really grand views unsurpassed by anything you will have seen before. You are able to request the train to stop for you at Newtondale Halt or only do part of the walk and pick the train up again at Levisham Station.

Walking from Levisham Station takes you away from Newtondale and across the North York Moors to visit the site of an ancient civilization, a monks fish pond and the Hole of Horcum with its fantasy and folklore.

It is always good to have an eating stop when walking and I can certainly recommend a couple of my favourite pubs for you to visit. The Horeshoe Inn at Levisham village is highly recommended and when you are near to Goathland you must stop at the Birch Hall Inn at Beck Hole. A quaint old Inn and a pretty little village in a deep hollow near the moors and railway. Ask for a Beckhole Butty, you will not be disappointed!

At the Northern end of the line is Grosmont. A village built on a hillside. The first train leaves Grosmont around ten o'clock in the morning but there is much activity before then. I advise you to go to Grosmont well before the departure time of the first train and take a walk along to the engine sheds. There is lots of hustle and bustle there as the engines build up a good head of steam before setting off. They take on coal and water, prepare the engine, do their safety checks and sort out any little problems before a hard days steaming to Goathland and back. There are a couple of walks from Grosmont, one along the now disused George Stephenson track to Goathland from where you can once again jump on the train to complete your journey.

Goathland is well known for its 'Heartbeat' connections and you might just see your favourite stars there doing a days filming. Take a walk through the village and see if you can spot Mostyn's Garage and the local pub, both used in the TV series. A little way out of the village on the Pickering road lies the farm used as Greengrass's lair, if you see it you will recognise it instantly by the junk piled all around. From Goathland Station you can walk to Beckhole and the Birch Hall Inn, have a wonderful Beck Hole Butty and spend the afternoon there. You can visit a waterfall by walking over the bridge then turning right at the public footpath sign which leads to Thomason Foss. Or you can walk all the way to Grosmont to catch the train.

Nearby Beck Hole is the old railway incline, where carriages were hauled up and down the slope on a rope. It was powered by water which was used as ballast . Almost a mile in length it has had its share of accidents, probably the most serious being on a frosty evening on the 13th of February 1864. The train having been detached the carriages would have been attached to a brake van which itself was attached to the rope. The carriages were then pushed over the incline in a controlled descent. On this fateful February day when only a few hundred yards down the incline the rope snapped and the carriages hurtled down the incline picking up terrific speed. The line curves to the right at the bottom to cross the beck. This was too much for the speeding carriages. They derailed killing two passengers and injuring fourteen others. Today you can walk the incline, but listen carefully and you might just hear the screams of the ghosts of the terrified passengers as they hurtle down the incline to their deaths!

ROUTE 1
ALONG THE ESK VALLEY

Take a walk to Grosmont and catch the train there or walk the return route to Goathland by using **Route 5** in this book, the choice is yours.

The Facts

Distance - 4 miles/6½km each way
Time - 2 hours or 3½ hours
Start - Goathland Station, grid ref. 837013
Map - OS Landranger 94 or OS Outdoor Leisure 27
Refreshment - Signals Buffet on Grosmont platform is highly recommended
Public Toilets - Goathland and Grosmont platforms
Guide Book - Walking around the North York Moors by J.Brian Beadle has similar walks. Available from the Pickering Railway Station Shop, Low Dalby Visitor Centre, Bookshops and Tourist Information Centres

Your Route

Leave Goathland Railway Station away from the village through the gate at the rear of the level crossing then turn immediately left. The path climbs at first parallel to the railway and beck then descends into Darnholme with superb views ahead. Bear slightly right away from the railway to a small footbridge. Keep on the obvious path towards the stepping stones - do not cross. Turn right here along a driveway at the public footpath sign. In a few yards the driveway bends to the right, turn left now to leave the drive onto a rough track. In a few yards cross the footbridge on the left to start a steep climb. There is a seat half way up, take a rest and admire the view then continue climbing to the top. Go left now over the stile at the gate and waymark. Soon pass through another gate, past a house and waymark then exit through a small gate. Take the grassy path nearest the wall now. Good views across the railway and Goathland to the moors. When the path splits keep on the right path nearest the wall. Soon you come to a waymark post. Go left here as directed onto a narrow path through the bracken, keep a sharp eye out in a few yards taking an even narrower path through the bracken on the left. The path falls and soon reaches another waymark post at a crossroad of tracks. Turn left here and descend through the bracken. Shortly cross a wide grassy path then keep descending through the bracken. Care now, this one is very steep and can be slippery. Bear right at the wall then keep right away from the bridge. Do not cross the footbridge over the river! Follow the fence round to the right then take care on a narrow path with a precipitous drop when climbing back onto the moor. Fol-

6

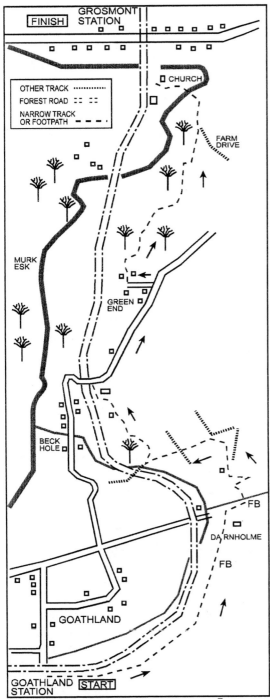

low the wall in front of you passing a farm then join a farm track. Follow this almost to the next farm then turn left towards the signpost opposite. Turn right at the sign to exit along the farm drive. At the road go right then in half a mile turn left to Green End. At Green End Farm turn right through two gates at the 'Bridleway' sign. Pass between a pair of stone gateposts then head for the hedged lane in front. A stone trod now appears. Soon go right at the sign for 'Footpath to Grosmont'. Descend into the wood then through a field and over a stile into a wood again. In a few yards cross a stile into a field turning sharp left. Leave the field across two stiles into another field keeping straight ahead. Soon over a stile and a bridge into the wood. You meet up with the stone trod again in the woods. Exit over a stile turning left into the field following the trod downhill to soon meet a farm drive. Bear left onto the drive then soon through a gate continuing downhill. Just before the ford go left over the footbridge, then left at the end up the steps. At the junction go left past the church then go right through a gate at the 'Rail Trail' sign to return to Grosmont and the path you started on.

ROUTE 2
A SCENIC WALK TO DARNHOLME AND BEYOND

Darnholme is only a couple of farms and a few houses situated adjacent to Goathland. The road to Darnholme leads to a pleasant picnic area. Eller Beck flows through Darnholme where the road is a ford and pedestrian stepping stones are provided. Darnholme has a little history for coal was found there, although of poor quality. There was a fulling mill on the beck and cloth was stretched out to dry on the moor. The last house on the hill was once the home of Tommy Leng, Cobbler.

The Facts

Distance - 2½ miles/4km
Time - 1½ hours
Start - Goathland Station, grid ref. 837013
Map - OS Landranger 94 or OS Outdoor Leisure 27
Refreshment - Light refreshment on the platform, cafe and pub in the village
Public Toilets - On the platform and in the village car park
Guide Book - Walking around Rosedale, Farndale & Hutton le Hole by J.Brian Beadle has similar walks. Available from Pickering Railway Station Shop, Low Dalby Visitor Centre, Bookshops and Tourist Information Centres.

Your Route

Leave Goathland Railway Station away from the village through the gate at the rear of the level crossing then turn immediately left. The path climbs at first parallel to the railway and beck then descends into Darnholme giving superb views of the railway and the surrounding area. Bear slightly right away from the railway to a small footbridge. Keep on the obvious path towards the stepping stones. Turn right here along a driveway at the public footpath sign. In a few yards the driveway bends to the right, turn left now to leave the drive onto a rough track. In a few yards cross the footbridge on the left to start a steep climb. There is a seat half way up, take a rest and admire the view then continue climbing to the top. Go left now over the stile at the gate and waymark. Soon through another gate, past a house and waymark then exit through a small gate. Take the grassy path nearest the wall now. Good views across the railway and Goathland to the moors. When the path splits keep on the right path nearest the wall. Soon you come to a waymark post. Go left here as directed onto a narrow path through the bracken, keep a sharp eye out in a few yards taking an even narrower path through the bracken on the left. The path falls and soon reaches another waymark post at a crossroad of tracks. Turn left here and descend through the bracken. Soon cross a wide grassy path then keep descending through the bracken. Care now, this one is very steep and can be slippery. Bear right at the wall then left under the railway and over Eller Beck on a footbridge. It is a steep climb now but it soon ends and you exit into a field over a stile. Still climbing, this field path can be very muddy at times but not for long as you cross a stile onto a drier path which leads to the road. At the road turn left, there is a wide grass verge and an old stone trod for you to walk on. At the crossroads turn right signed 'Local traffic only'. Continue along towards the village then turn left at the junction towards the shops. Walk past the shops to return to the railway station.

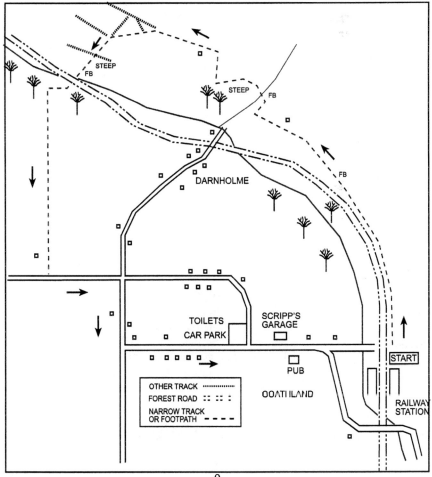

ROUTE 3
WATER, WATER EVERYWHERE!

S itting in the sun outside the Birch Hall Inn eating your Beckhole Butty and drinking a pint of good old Black Sheep Brewery ale is no excuse for not walking any further. (But this is arguable!) Yet to come are a couple of stiff climbs, a walk along the beck side and a grand waterfall. So eat and drink up and let's be on our way!

The Facts

Distance - 4 miles/6.4km

Time - 2 hours

Start - Goathland Station, grid ref.. 837013

Map - OS Landranger 94 or OS Outdoor Leisure 27

Refreshment - Along the way have a Beckhole Butty (highly recommended) at the Birch Hall Inn at Beckhole or a snack at the Prudom House Tea Rooms near the Mallyan Spout.

Public Toilets - On the platform and in the car park en-route

Guide Book - Walking around Ryedale, Pickering & Helmsley by J.Brian Beadle has similar walks. Available from the Pickering Railway Station Shop, Low Dalby Visitor Centre, Bookshops and Tourist Information Centres

Your Route

L eave the railway station up the hill towards the village of Goathland. Pass the pub on your left and Scripp's Garage on your right, both are used in the Heartbeat series on television. A little further along turn right at the sign-post for 'Darnholme and Beckhole'. Pass the car park and toilets then go left into a field at the sign for 'Grosmont Rail Trail'. You are now on the track of the old railway at the top of the incline.

Continue downhill to the road. Cross the road and keep straight ahead down the old railway incline. Carriages were hauled up and down this incline. After a pleasant walk pass through a gate into the grounds of Incline Cottage. Pass the cottage then if you are going to the Birch Hall Inn for one of their superb sandwiches ignore the waymark and sign 'To The Mallyan' on your left and continue along bearing right at the sign for Beckhole. In a few yards you reach the village and the Inn. Return to this point and take the path signed to the Mallyan. Shortly the path climbs steeply, at the top there are good views be-hind you.

Pass through a couple of gates and a field before descending down to the Beck. Soon you see a signpost. To visit the Mallyan Spout waterfall go straight ahead. Be very careful the rocks are treacherous. Return to the signpost after visiting the waterfall and walk uphill in the direction of Goathland. It is a long stiff climb but eventually you reach the Mallyan Hotel at the top. Go left onto the road here passing or dropping in at the Prudom House Tea Rooms. Opposite the tea rooms turn right at the footpath sign for 'Abbots House'. Just past 'The Beacon' guest house go straight ahead through a gate into a field. Keep straight ahead at the next gate/stile and shortly another stile. Soon the path goes right over a footbridge and stone stile then in a few yards goes left over a stile into a caravan park. Bear right through the caravan park to eventually reach onto the old railway track. Go left here and walk back to Goathland. At the road turn right and down the hill to the railway station.

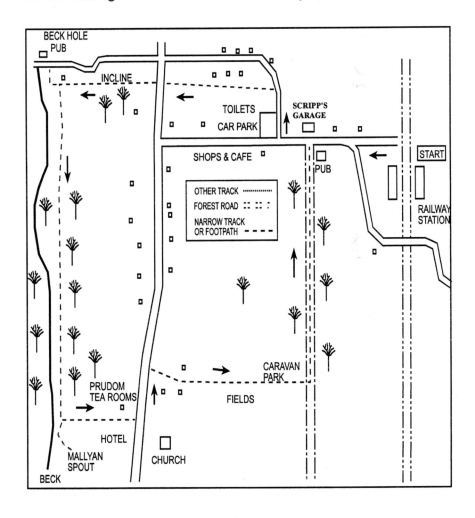

ROUTE 4
ALONG STEPHENSON'S RAILWAY TRACK

This scenic route uses the old railway track which was opened in 1836 by George Stephenson as a horse drawn tramway. After many successful years the line was bought by "Mr. Railway" himself, George Hudson in 1845. He converted the line to carry steam engines and used this track until 1865.

The Facts

Distance - 5 miles/8km

Time - 2 hours

Start - Grosmont Station, grid ref.. 828053

Map - OS Landranger 94 or OS Outdoor Leisure 27

Refreshment - Along the way have a Beckhole Butty
at the Birch Hall Inn at Beckhole
or pop into the Signals Buffet on the platform at Grosmont,
the freshly baked Cornish pasties are delicious

Public Toilets - On the platform or in the village

Guide Book - Walking around Rosedale, Farndale and Hutton
le Hole by J.Brian Beadle has similar walks. Available from the
Pickering Railway Station Shop, Low Dalby Visitor Centre,
Bookshops and Tourist Information Centres

Your Route

Leave the platform turning left over the level crossing. Immediately over the crossing take the path on the right signed to 'Loco shed and Goathland'. Cross the bridge over the Murk Esk then turn left uphill past the school and church signed as 'Rail Trail'. Exit through a gate turning right along the 'Rail Trail'. Uphill through a gate then left through another gate at the sign for 'Goathland, Rail Trail'. Downhill now past the engine sheds and workshop on the left through a couple of gates to turn right onto Stephenson's old railway track. Keep straight ahead at the houses and go through the gate. Soon you will see a small plaque with details about the old railway. Keep straight ahead passing the odd bridge and field or two to enter the woods soon bearing right over another bridge over the river, ignoring the steps on the left! Pass through a small gate and at the sign keep straight ahead signed to 'Goathland Rail Trail'. Shortly you will see the houses of Beck Hole coming into view on the left. The path splits here, bear left, cross the stile and walk to the village. In the village go right to the Birch Hall Inn if you are in need of refreshment, if continuing with the walk turn left and climb the steep hill out of the village.

Look back as you climb there are great views across the village and along the precipitous valley towards the Mallyan Spout. Keep climbing over a railway bridge then follow the road round to the left. Continue along this quiet road for some way until you meet a junction on the left. Go down this road to the houses of Green End. At Green End Farm turn right through two gates at the 'Bridleway' sign. Pass between a pair of stone gateposts then head for the hedged lane in front of you. A stone trod now appears. Soon go right at the sign for 'Footpath to Grosmont'. Descend into the wood then through a field

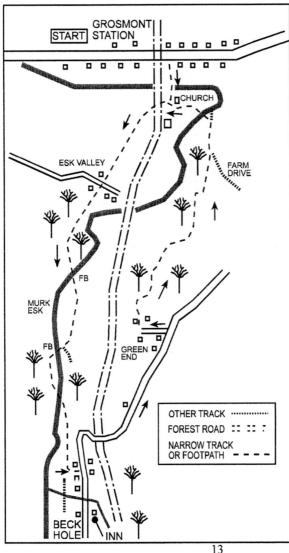

and over a stile into a wood again. In a few yards cross a stile into a field turning sharp left. Leave the field across two stiles into another field keeping straight ahead. Soon over a stile and a bridge into the wood. You meet up with the stone trod again in the wood. Exit over a stile turning left into the field following the trod downhill to soon meet a farm drive. Bear left onto the drive then soon through a gate continuing downhill. Just before the ford go left over the foot-bridge, then left at the end up some steps. At the junction go left past the church then right through a gate at the 'Rail Trail' sign to return to Grosmont and the path you started on.

ROUTE 5
AN EASY WALK TO GOATHLAND

The walk from Grosmont to Goathland is along George Stephenson's 1936 railway line. As you approach Beck Hole you are in the area of the Beckhole Iron Works of the 1860's. It is hard to believe now walking through such beautiful scenery that it was a bustling industrial place with a blast furnace roaring away. Before the ironworks there was a fulling mill nearby in the early 1700's. In the village, women sat at their spinning wheels and one chap collected the wool not suitable for spinning to make felt with.

If you would like a longer walk this one can be combined with route one, Goathland to Grosmont making a round trip of eight miles, but is a little more trying. My choice would be to stop off at Beckhole and have a Beckhole Butty at the Birch Hall Inn then a leisurely walk to Goathland, take a look at the old cars and motorcycles at 'Heartbeat's 'Mostyn's Garage' alias the Goathland Garage, then a cup of tea at Goathland Station before catching the train home.

The Facts

Distance - 4 miles/6½km, linear route
Time - 2 hours
Start - Grosmont Station, grid ref. 828053
Map - OS Landranger 94 or Outdoor Leisure 27
Refreshment - Plenty of choice in Goathland,
The Birch Hall Inn at Beckhole
Public Toilets - On the platforms, Grosmont near bridge,
Goathland car park
Guide Book - Walking around the North York Moors by
J.Brian Beadle has similar walks. Available from the Pickering
Railway Station Shop, Low Dalby Visitor Centre,
Bookshops and Tourist Information Centres

Your Route

Leave the platform turning left over the level crossing. Immediately over the crossing take the path on the right signed to 'Loco shed and Goathland'. Cross the bridge over the Murk Esk then turn left uphill past the school and church signed as 'Rail Trail'. Exit through a gate turning right along the 'Rail Trail'. Uphill through a gate then left through another gate at the sign for 'Goathland, Rail Trail'. Downhill now past the engine sheds and workshop on the left through a couple of gates to turn right onto Stephenson's old railway

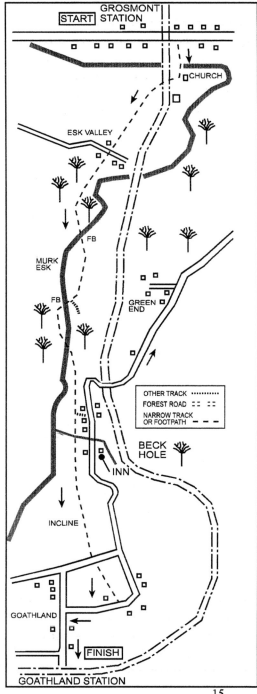

track. Keep straight ahead at the houses and go through the gate. Keep straight ahead passing the odd bridge and field or two to enter the woods soon bearing right over another bridge over the river, ignoring the steps on the left uphill into the woods! Pass through a small gate and at the sign keep straight ahead signed to 'Goathland Rail Trail'. Shortly you will see the houses of Beck Hole coming into view on the left. *The path splits here, bear left, cross the stile and walk to the village turning right to the Birch Hall Inn if you are in need of refreshment. To return to the path to Goathland take the gate almost opposite the Inn signed 'Bridleway to Thackside and Rail Trail' then left through the next gate towards the incline.* If you are not taking refreshment continue past Beck Hole to cross the bridge. Keep straight ahead past Incline Cottage to walk up the incline. At the top cross the road and continue up the incline through a field. Exit the field through a gate turning right past the toilets. At the junction turn right for the village shops or left to Mostyn's Garage and that cup of tea at Goathland Station.

ROUTE 6
A WOODLAND WALK FROM PICKERING STATION

This pleasant woodland walk has a choice of return routes. One climbs high through the wood and returns to Pickering through the town, the other crosses the railway to return along a forest road to the level crossing at Newbridge then back to the station along the road.

The Facts

Distance - 6 miles/9.6km, either route
Time - 3 hours
Start - Pickering Station, grid ref. 797842
Map - OS Landranger 100 or Outdoor Leisure 27
Refreshment - Tea Rooms at the station and in the town
Public Toilets - Pickering Railway Station
Guide Book - Walking around Ryedale, Pickering & Helmsley by J.Brian Beadle has similar walks. Available from the Pickering Railway Station Shop, Low Dalby Visitor Centre, Bookshops and Tourist Information Centres

Your Route

Leave the station by the main entrance and turn right onto the footpath. At the crossroads go right past the Mulberries Coffee Shop, over the bridge and past Beck Isle Museum. Up the hill then sharp right. Where the road goes sharp left leave it and go straight ahead along Beacon Park. At the top of the road go right along a narrow path. You have fine views of Pickering Castle from here. At the stiles go left and soon bear right down a muddy slope into a field. Left here then through a small gate past the caravan park. Shortly cross a stile into a field. Straight ahead now to the large oak trees then bear right across the field to a gate. Through the gate keep straight ahead ignoring all other tracks to eventually arrive at the gate to Rock Cottage. Keep straight on past the cottage and studio then through more gates into a field. Exit the field turning right past the front of the cottages, cross the railway track with care and continue along to the road. Cross the road and walk along the drive to Lowther House passing between the buildings soon to enter Pickering Woods. Follow the path through the woods for some time eventually exiting the wood over a stile into a field. Turn right and follow the path all the way to the end of the field then re-enter the wood. In about a mile the path splits, this is your choice of routes for the return journey - *To return on the lower route to Newbridge crossing go left over the bridge and railway. At the forest road turn left. This takes you all the way back to Newbridge, (take care through the*

16

works yard). Follow the road over the crossing back to the station. - Alternatively follow the path right to soon climb steeply, cross a wider path right then left still climbing, cross another wide path still climbing. At the top bear right into the wood then in a few yards exit the wood through a gate and go right. Follow the obvious path through several gates and fields then look out for the path going left across the middle of the field opposite an old wooden gate on the right. At the trees cross the stiles and keep straight ahead across the field. Soon follow the path straight ahead to a housing estate. Cross the road here still straight ahead through the houses to the main road. Bear right then right again at the castle sign. Follow this road until it ends at a 'T' junction. You have a choice now, right for the castle, left then right into the town, straight ahead down Brant Hill to the station.

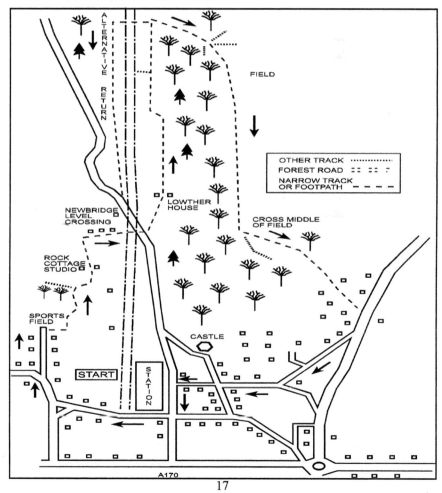

ROUTES 7 & 8
TWO WALKS FROM THE NEWTONDALE HALT

Newtondale is embraced with steep sided cliffs and rock faces, left behind when the dale was gouged out by the rushing waters from a huge ice-age lake as the ice melted. The first walk visits Needle Point, a high vantage viewpoint on the edge of precipitous cliffs. The footpath crosses the face of one of these cliffs and the views are varied and breathtaking. This is not a walk suitable for families as there are sheer unguarded cliffs for most of the walk. The traverse of the cliff face is not difficult but again there is a steep unguarded drop to be aware of. Good footwear is essential on this walk and is recommended for all the other walks. Route two is a low level walk on forest roads. **You must tell the Guard you wish to alight and be picked up at Newtondale Halt or the train will not stop.**

The Facts
Distance - 3½ miles/5.6km. both routes are the same distance
Time - 2 hours
Start - Newtondale Halt, grid ref. 835948
Map - OS Landranger 94 or OS Outdoor Leisure 27
Refreshments - None
Public Toilets - What, in a forest? You'll have to improvise!
Guide Book - Walking the Ridges & Riggs of the North York Moors by J.Brian Beadle has similar walks. Available from the Pickering Railway Station Shop, Low Dalby Visitor Centre, Bookshops and Tourist Information Centres.

Route 7 - Needle Point

Leave the platform turning left downhill, past an information board then bear right uphill to a forest road. Right now onto the road for a pleasant walk towards Needle Point. When the road splits go right downhill then shortly as the road rises turn left at the sign for 'Needle Point & Newtondale Well'. It is a hard climb on the narrow path through the forest but soon you arrive at a sign directing you to 'Newtondale Well'. Visit the well if you like then return to this point. Continue along the path across the cliff face then shortly take an acute left turn onto the escarpment edge path. Follow this path to Needle Point and enjoy grand views across Newtondale. Continue along to eventually meet a wide grassy track. Go left here to soon rejoin the escarpment edge path. At the stony forest road go left, then in about 20 yards go left again onto a wide track which soon narrows. After some time you arrive at a crossroad of tracks. Take the first track on the left, signed 'Return to Newtondale Halt'. It is a tricky descent at times if wet and where the path forks keep right. Soon you complete the descent and arrive at a forest road. Turn left now to return to Newtondale Halt. The entrance to Newtondale Halt is sometimes hard to detect. Look for the bulrush pond on your left, a few yards past the pond go right along a wide track to return to the platform.

Route 8 - Raper's Farm Picnic Area

Leave Newtondale Halt platform as in route 1 but at the forest road go left. Continue along the forest road keeping left at the fork. In about one mile the road bends right and climbs to meet the forest drive. Turn right here, watch out for traffic. Soon you pass Raper's Farm, the picnic area is straight ahead in the field. Turn right past the picnic area leaving the forest drive and descend along a wide forest road. At the junction bear left to return on the same road you started on. Look out for the bulrush pond on the left then go right to return to the platform.

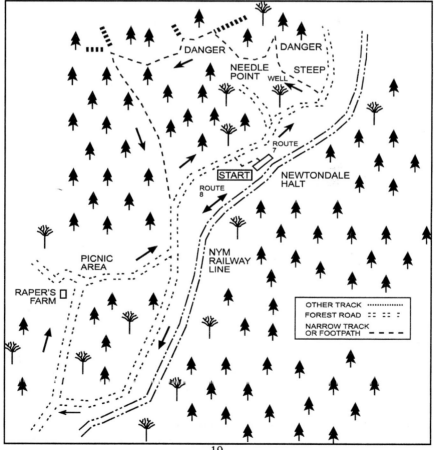

ROUTE 9
SCENIC STEAM IN NEWTONDALE

Take your camera with you on this superb scenic walk through Cropton Forest. You will find lots of interest as you walk through the forest which is home to beautiful Newtondale.

The Facts

Distance - 8½ miles/13.6km
Time - 4 hours
Start - Levisham Station, grid ref. 818910
Map - OS Landranger 94 or OS Outdoor Leisure 27
Refreshment - Only on special weekends on the platform
Public Toilets - On the platform
Guide Book - Walking in Dalby, the Great Yorkshire Forest by J.Brian Beadle has similar walks. Available from the Pickering Railway Station Shop, Low Dalby Visitor Centre, Bookshops and Tourist Information Centres

Your Route

Leave the platform and head off into the forest along the forest drive road for one mile until you reach a pair of holiday cottages, called 'Platelayers Cottages'. Just past the cottages turn left uphill on a forest road at the sign for Raindale. In a couple of hundred yards turn right uphill at the blue waymark. This is a narrow path and can be muddy for a short time if wet. Enter a field through a gate keeping straight ahead close to the fence on the right. Follow the fence left and uphill towards the house. When the fence turns to the right leave it and cross diagonally right uphill to a gap in the hedge in the top right hand corner of the field, then in a few yards exit through a small gate turning right onto the farm drive. Climb gently then enter the forest through a gate. Keep straight ahead until you come to a crossroad of tracks at a severe left bend. Go right here onto a wide grassy forest track soon passing a blue waymark. Keep straight ahead on this track until it kinks right then left then soon leaves the forest. Turn right onto a wide forest road now. Walk for about half a mile until you pass through a double bend. Ignore the blue waymarks then in a couple of hundred yards look for a grassy track on the right leaving the road at an angle. Take this path into the forest, cross a wider forest path to follow the waymark straight ahead on the grass track. Eventually the path narrows and descends to a very pretty steep sided griff, take care here! Cross a very small stream then climb on the obvious track to soon join the forest drive road. Turn right now down hill and at Rapers' Farm Picnic Site where the road takes a severe right turn leave the road to go left onto a forest road to descend towards the railway. When you eventually join another forest road go left. Half a mile from the start ignore the wide farm road on your right and keep walking until you reach a wide grassy track going right and downhill just past the bulrush pond on the left. Cross the rickety stile alongside the large gate and pass under the bridge at the railway station. Turn left along a path between railway and beck. The path takes you over two stiles and a footbridge then climbs steeply into the forest. Soon cross the stile on the right out of the forest and continue to climb, very steeply at times and over a wooden staircase. At the top, turn right onto a path along the escarpment. Soon the path goes left to join a wider track going right. Continue along this wide track passing Skelton Tower on your right. Continue straight ahead to join the road to Levisham Station. Go right at the road to descend to the station.

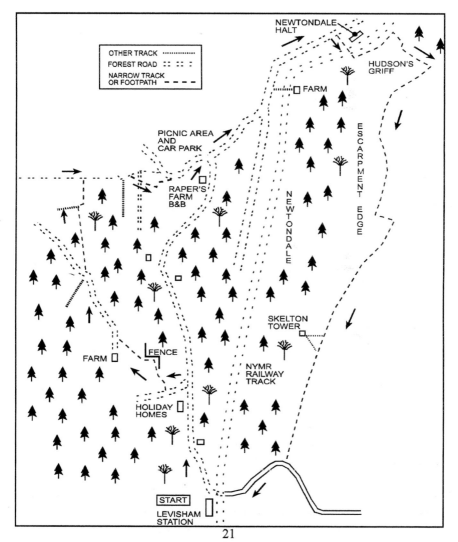

ROUTE 10
LEVISHAM AND THE HORSE SHOE INN

It is a hard, long climb from Levisham Station all the way onto Levisham Moor but I think you will agree that the grand views from the top are worth the effort. Looking across Newtondale you will see the hill top village of Newton on Rawcliffe opposite you. To the north there are good views of Cropton Forest and Newtondale across to the North York Moors above Goathland. To the east more super views past the Hole of Horcum and the great forest of Dalby.

The Facts
Distance - 3½ miles/5.6km
Time - 2 hours
Start - Levisham Station, grid ref.. 818910
Map - OS Landranger 94 or OS Outdoor Leisure 27
Refreshment - Levisham, the Horseshoe Inn
Public Toilets - On the platfrom
Guide Book - Walking to Abbeys, Castles
& Churches by J.Brian Beadle has similar
walks. Available from Pickering Railway
Station Shop, Low Dalby Visitor Centre,
Bookshops and Tourist Information Centres.

Your Route

Leave the station away from the forest to walk along the road up a very steep hill. Where the road sweeps severely to the right ignore the bridleway sign to leave the road straight ahead and walk across the grass towards a seat half way up the hill opposite. At the seat bear left across the face of the hillside. At the top bear slightly right to the

wall then follow the wall straight ahead. Soon you see a post of waymarks. Go right here following the wall to walk across the field to a gate and a stone stile. Cross the stile and follow the farm road until it meets a tarmac road. Keep straight ahead here to descend to Levisham Village. The Horseshoe Inn is on the left. Pass the Inn or call for refreshment, then in a few yards turn right past the chapel and between some rather pretty cottages. Soon, after leaving the vicinity of the cottages the road bends acutely to the left. Go straight ahead here over the stile into a field near the public footpath sign. Continue across the field and cross another stile into another field. The exit to this field is over a stile in the distant right hand corner. Bear right over the stile along a narrow path across the middle of the hillside. The track bends left, then right around the hill then follows a wider track downhill with wonderful views across Newtondale and Levisham Station.

At the bottom of the slope you will see a signpost. Walk towards the gate in the direction of 'station'. Cross the stile near the gate bear right then downhill to a small gate at the bottom of the field. Pass through the gate into the wood and follow this path to soon exit onto the road turning left to return to Levisham Station.

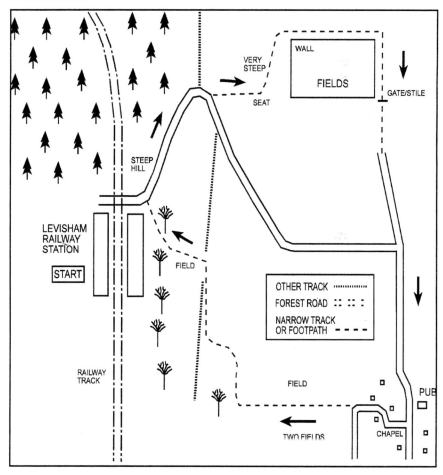

ROUTE 11

SKELTON TOWER

This walk takes in the wild moors and gentle valleys of North Yorkshire to the folly known as Skelton Tower. Levisham is a pretty moorland village with the Horse Shoe Inn as its centrepiece. The walk to Skelton Tower gives glimpses of some of the most majestic scenery on the moors. The steam railway runs along Newtondale every hour. George Stephenson opened a railway in the dale in 1836 although the coaches were initially drawn by horses. The railway was in operation for over 100 years until closed in the Beeching era. Then reopened as the North Yorkshire Moors Railway some years later.

The Facts

Distance - 6 miles/10km

Time - 3 hours

Start - Levisham Station, grid ref. 818910

Map - OS Landranger 94 or OS Outdoor Leisure 27

Refreshment - Levisham, the Horseshoe Inn

Public Toilets - On the platform

Guide Book - Short Walks around Yorkshire's Coast & Countryside by J.Brian Beadle has similar walks. Available from Pickering Railway Station Shop, Low Dalby Visitor Centre, Bookshops and Tourist Information Centres.

Your Route

Leave the station turning left to enter the forest along the forest drive road. Walk along the forest road for about a mile. At the sign for 'Newtondale Halt (via moors)' go right downhill and over a bridge. Cross the railway line with care and take the footpath which is signed up the hill. Half way up the hill turn left and follow the path to the top of the hill. *Look out for several large, flat stones with hollowed out centres, these are querns. They were used hundreds of years ago for grinding corn.* The path is undefined now but head over the moor to the trees and wall on the left. Follow the wall for a couple of hundred yards then turn right over the moor until you reach a wide well defined track.

Join the track going left and on the horizon you will see the ruins of Skelton Tower. The view from the tower over Newtondale is stunning, if you are fortunate you might see a steam train puffing its way along the dale. Retrace your steps from the tower, cross the track that you came on and head for the path leading up the opposite hillside. Once over the crest of the hill follow the path as far as a stone wall. Bear left down the hill into a gully then slightly right to

arrive at Dundale Pond. Leave the pond by the track up the hill on the right signposted to Levisham Braygate.

Follow the track over the moor to a gate in the corner of a field and leave by the stone stile into a lane. This eventually meets a road, if you wish to visit the Horseshoe Inn go left, to return to the Railway Station go right and down the steep hill. Follow the road all the way to the station and enjoy fine views across Newtondale.

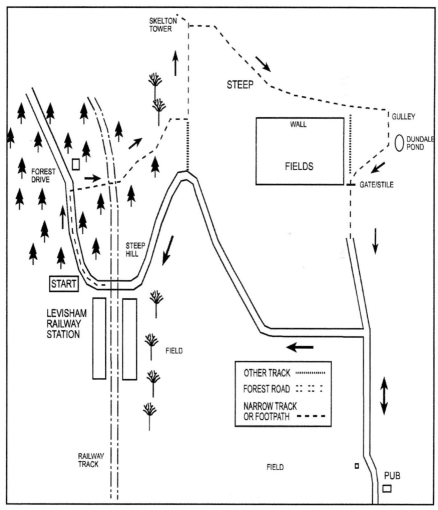

ROUTE 12
FOLKLORE & FANTASY

Near the start of the walk you pass the remains of a folly on the edge of the cliff overlooking breathtaking Newtondale. The footpath continues along the edge of this great dale before climbing onto the moor to overlook the Hole of Horcum. Return on the path which passes the site of an iron age settlement, (look for the information plaque) and a Monk's pond. Folklore says that giant Horcum had an argument with the Devil near here and scooped up a handful of earth to throw at him from the moor, forming the Hole of Horcum. The earth landed not far away and is said to be a hill called Blakey Topping. The truth is the hole was formed by the escape of water during the ice age!

The Facts

Distance - 7 miles/11.2km

Time - 3 hours

Start - Levisham Station, grid ref. 818910

Map - OS Landranger 94 or OS Outdoor Leisure 27

Refreshments - The Horseshoe Inn at Levisham near the end of the walk

Public toilets - On the platform

Guide Book - Walking around the North York Moors by J.Brian Beadle has similar walks. Available from the Pickering Railway Station Shop, Low Dalby Visitor Centre, Bookshops and Tourist Information Centres

Your Route

Leave the station turning right up the road and a very steep hill. Soon the road flattens out and when it goes severely right you must go left onto the moor in the direction of the bridleway sign onto a wide, rutted track. Shortly you arrive at a wooden signpost. Keep straight ahead here leaving the bridleway to follow the sign for footpath. Soon the fantasy of the Reverend Skelton, Skelton Tower comes into view, a broken down stone building. Walk past the tower to reach the escarpment edge of Newtondale. The views into this deep gorge are stunning. The gorge was formed when ice age water escaped from a lake further along the moor and swept along at great pace gouging out Newtondale. The North Yorkshire Moors steam railway now runs along the dale but not at any great pace! Keep on the wide track away from Skelton Tower and Newtondale for 2 miles until it bends to the right following the contour of the hill on the right. In front of you at the road is the Saltersgate Inn if you wish to take refreshment there. Keep bearing right as the wide track disappears into a narrow one then climb up the hill side to almost meet the road at a hairpin bend. Bear right now, here would be a good place to eat your sandwiches whilst enjoying the fantastic view. Continue along a wide track over the top of the moor with good views to the left into the Hole of Horcum. On the right look out for the two plaques describing the Iron Age settlement. Where the track dips you will see on the right the first of two ponds, Seavey Pond, although it is often dry in summer. Soon the track sweeps down to Dundale Pond which was given to the Monks, read the plaque there giving its history. Leave Dundale Pond in the direction of 'Station'. The path climbs to a waymark post. Keep straight ahead here along the line of the wall. At the next set of waymarks enjoy the superb view then go left down the hill in the direction of the yellow waymark to the road and back to the station.

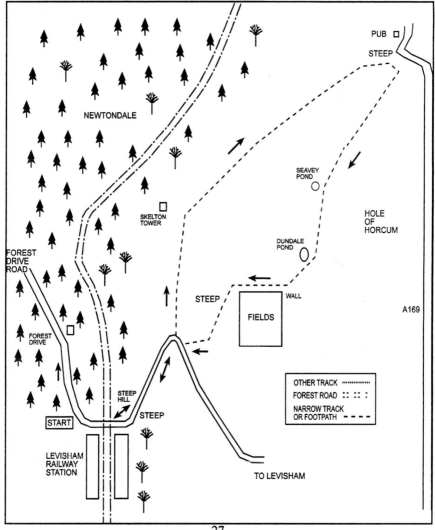

TRAILBLAZER BOOKS
CYCLING BOOKS
Mountain Biking around the Yorkshire Dales
Mountain Biking the Easy Way
Mountain Biking in North Yorkshire
Mountain Biking on the Yorkshire Wolds
Mountain Biking for Pleasure
Mountain Biking in the Lake District
Mountain Biking around Ryedale, Wydale & the North York Moors
Exploring Ryedale, Moor & Wold by Bicycle (Road cycling)
Beadle's Bash - 100 mile challenge route for Mountain Bikers

WALKING BOOKS
Walking in Heartbeat Country
Walking in Captain Cook's Footsteps
Walking the Riggs & Ridges of the North York Moors
Short Walks around Yorkshire's Coast & Countryside
Walking on the Yorkshire Coast
Walking to Abbeys, Castles & Churches
Walking around the North York Moors
Walking around Scarborough, Whitby & Filey
Walking to Crosses on the North York Moors
Walks from the Harbour (Scarborough)
Walking in Dalby, the Great Yorkshire Forest
Ten Scenic Walks around Rosedale, Farndale & Hutton le Hole
Twelve Scenic Walks from the North Yorkshire Moors Railway
Twelve Scenic Walks around Ryedale, Pickering & Helmsley
Twelve Scenic Walks around the Yorkshire Dales

DOING IT YOURSELF SERIES
Make & Publish Your Own Books

OTHER BOOKS
The Trailblazer Guide to Crosses & Stones on the North York Moors
Curious Goings on in Yorkshire

For more information please visit our web site:
www.trailblazerbooks.co.uk